Scent of an Angel

pk davies

JOYFUL LIFE MASTERY BOOKS

Copyright © 2021 by P.K. Davies

ISBN: 978-1-7770525-8-4

All rights reserved. No part of this publication may be reproduced, distributed, or transmitted in any form or by any means, including photocopying, recording, or other electronic or mechanical methods, without the prior written permission of Joyful Life Mastery, except by a reviewer, who may quote brief passages in a review.

For information about special discounts for bulk purchases, please contact Joyful Life Mastery at JoyfulLifeMastery@gmail.com.

Book Website and Newsletter:

www.joyfullifemastery.com

Socia Media:

https://www.facebook.com/joyfullifemastery

for my angels

Table of Contents

welcome..1

innocence - child of the universe

i know i saw you.. 7

dreams of spun sugar....................................... 10

freedom 13

disenchantment - world of shadows

noise 17

free hugs 21

angel rising... 27

hope

today's prayer 31

the pink feather.. 33

surrender - avatar

angel song 39

breath of the angels 41

love letter... 45

the blessing 49

thank you 51

about the author 52

Also by PK Davies:... 53

Join Me! 54

welcome

Ever since childhood, I've been fascinated by the idea of angels, fairies, mermaids, elves, and unseen magical spirit guides.

Elemental or celestial beings who transcend time and religion.

I've been fascinated by the human yearning for the divine and the magical.

And to know that we are guided by spirit in whichever way is meaningful for us.

As an adult, I now believe that angels are everywhere in our lives - loving beings who come into our lives to offer guidance, comfort and love. Sometimes they appear through people we know. And other times as strangers or nudges towards unexplainable healing circumstances or transformative experiences.

Religion and spirituality can help, and yet to some of us, they don't always hold the answers to life that truly satisfy.
Why do tragedies occur? What happens when our heartfelt prayers aren't answered?
Is anyone really out there?

I don't have these answers either. My best guesses are just that – or a hopeful belief in one spiritual tradition or another. I know what I do believe on some levels, given the mysteries that I've experienced. That there is something loving and vast that encompasses us all.

But maybe having different experiences and beliefs is what Life entails.

Perhaps our journey involves looking for meaning, and the hero's journey lies in finding it.
Looking towards positive changes in our human connections and within society.

Righting wrongs when possible and without harm.

Perhaps it's about drawing our attention back to living life how best we can in any given moment.

Maybe there's not a single religion or spiritual mindset that answers *all* our questions.

Maybe there's a glimmer of truth in all of them. Meant to be handpicked through, the truly meaningful ideas for each of us plucked out with care and gently placed together in a shimmering box of Life's Comfort that we can turn to as we need and desire.

Perhaps angels and spirit guides exist.
Perhaps they are here for a reason unknown to us.
And perhaps there is nothing out there other than ourselves.

Perhaps we have to make our way as best we can.
Rising from tragedies together to live another day with hope and meaning.

Rebirthing a fresh innocence for life with each new morning in the face of that which can pull us down. Living in the moment by really feeling it with all our senses.

Perhaps angelic or godly energy is a *state of be-ing*, divine energy in free flow, rather than a Being. The energetic expression of Love.
If there is one redeeming quality on this Earth that I truly believe in, it is the healing nature of human connection with our shared pull towards compassion and growth.

And so...
Here's to the expansion of our personal and universal compassion.
Here's to us connecting with each other from the heart.
And here's to each of us finding our way together on this blue-green gem of a planet.

These little poems are a sharing from my heart to yours. A way of making sense of Life and our connection to healing transformation through various forms, including our own. And, yes, through angelic guides that transcend religion.

I thank you for joining me here and now.

With love,

P.K. Davies

innocence – child of the universe

i know i saw you

i remember

your face

your smile

i loved it

sunshine

behind you

you looked down at me

even then i saw

your compassion

your loving eyes

that swaddled me close

warm

there was softness

i exist

i am

am i love?

who am i?

what am i?

am i a game?

where do i end and you begin?

are you a picture that moves?

a dream

that came to me on a sunny day?

I see

your hair floating free

i love

your smile

are those wings behind you?

                                        someone told me

                                        you were a stranger

                                        who looked into my pram

                                        as we went for a stroll

but i know

that i saw you

i remember

dreams of spun sugar

motes of sunshine in the sky

dance with joyful glee

the glitter of your infinite sigh

floats aloft carefree

clouds that float with hints of blush

cosmic candy floss

the setting sun gleams sweet and lush

with universal gloss

how will you next bare your self

through time and history

in faerie form or forest elf

or mermaid mystery

i dare not look away at all

in case of magic missed

my senses gape around in thrall

imagination kissed

i lie bewitched upon the earth

bathing in the dream

looking up with childish mirth

joyfully a-gleam

i know not where you'll next appear

but i'll be on my toes

ready for the magic here

the universal shows

freedom

i throw that ball

against the wall

i feel your energy

free of strife

full of life

crisp vitality

as i run

full of fun

carried by the wind

i harness verve

without reserve

your soaring essence winged

disenchantment – world of shadows

noise

from all around

i hear the sounds

there's so much empty noise

i lie in bed

in my head

tranquility destroyed

i just don't know

the way to go

i feel so lost inside

too many rules

turn us to fools

our instincts are denied

connection dies

perfection lies

and we can only hide

                                    i feel alone

                                              are you still out there?

can you hear me?

                                                            hello?

i need someone to hear me

                                                       PLEASE

please

years later...

free hugs

you needed a hug

i could tell

but i could not

share one with you

                                                not then

i was far away

hidden

in my thoughts

and my fears

i'm sorry

i would have liked to have hugged you

i heard your sigh from afar

i sensed your loneliness too

don't we all need a hug

from time to time?

i think...sometimes...hugs are infused with the magical gift of love

just kidding

                                                                             not really

well

maybe i too need a hug sometimes

but i don't want to say that

i won't ask

it might look needy

and we all know

i'm not needy

we're not needy

right?

                                              okay, fine

breathe

let's just be for a moment

what were we talking about?

i've forgotten already

                                            so, do you?

need a hug, that is?

are there unshed tears?

a yearning deep inside?

for connection?

                    a sadness that you cannot name

                                        it's okay

you don't have to say anything

i understand

it's weird

for all of us

most of us can't anyway

in a world of masks

and six foot spaces

hugs aren't allowed yet

                          maybe we all could from afar?

alright - today look down at your arms

yes, yours

those arms that have cradled a baby

or an animal

                                   with such tenderness

those arms that hold boundless compassion

your hands, that play games and music with such innocence

your fingers, that write letters with hope

that gently wiped away someone's tears

                    i would be honored if you embrace me back

i'm thinking of you now

and sending you countless hugs

not a wish

or carried on a prayer

in my mind's eye, i hold you gently

i feel your heart

beating wildly against mine

seeking to make sense of it all

                                             it's okay

we're in this together

embracing all that is

this life

these bodies

        may this energy between us

              this hug

         burst into a thousand stars

           of light and magic

                        so be it

                        so it is

angel rising

shrouded in the shadows

too long have i lain in this place

hiding from the light of repose

guarding this frozen space

i cannot feel this heart that shattered

emotions too fierce to release

recoiling from all that ever mattered

held bound in eternal unease

my starving gaze breaks the witchery

    and drinks the magic of your mystery

        the hunger in my soul of infamy

            yearns for your angelic divinity

the light breaks through, pure and limitless

    as i rise from this tainted chrysalis

and now i know the darkness diffusing

    were the fears of my own choosing

hope

today's prayer

when it feels like my heart is in tatters

    from the senseless pain in the world

    i tell myself what really matters

there's still love on this earth, unfurled

love that grows

love that embraces

love that flows

love that graces

today, i will share a smile

today, i will message a friend

today, i will hug my child

today, i will enmity suspend

today, i will illuminate kindness

today, i will strive to unite

today, i will enhance my brightness

and embrace compassion and light

the pink feather

i asked for a sign

a magical quest

a little pink feather

a small final test

this way i'd know

one way or another

if i'd just imagined

this fanciful bother

i went for a walk

all senses alert

primed to unlock

ripe to exert

and yet as i strolled

my hopes raised once more

my smile all controlled

and eyes on the floor

i came across nothing

no feathers a-blush

i found myself cussing

hope newly crushed

at work i sat saddened

and bored out of mind

memories now blackened

and faith resigned

a tap on the glass

i turned to the sill

a peregrine with sass

fluttered its quill

it looked in at me

for hours galore

did not even flee

when colleagues took score

and when they had left

and we were alone

it puffed up its chest

with intent unknown

and there on its chest

for just me to see

lay feathers a-breast

all blush pink esprit

surrender – avatar

angel song

i hear the sound of your voice

trickling into my heart

i try to hold it far aside

but you have this down to an art

how is it that you always know

just the right things to say?

words that soften all my edges

and chase the shadows away

melodies made of satiny silk

rich with milk and honey

turning off my burdened mind

from thoughts of time is money

you carry me into your silvery world

with the strength of your voice and sound

i feel the beating of your wings

your hair around me unbound

breath of the angels

your breath floats upon the winds

scattered by mother earth

sacred breezes harnessing

the power of rebirth

i draw you in with potent gusts

aching for vitality

burning up the dark profane

to create a new reality

the gentle wisps of your spirit

embrace me in the mists

so gently and caressingly

like sweet lovers' trysts

i wait for all your mighty brawn

to slay sadness underpinned

yet, you whisper in my ear

deliverance lies within

call for us and we shall hear

we exist through time and space

we're around you in so many forms

and in the familiar face

reach for your beloved ones

remember you're never alone

we work in wondrous ways, my love

ask and the path will be shown

fear within is mixed with wonder

i sense your might immortal

the power that you wield with ease

rising to the cosmic portal

for you are me and i am you

we rest in this embrace

connecting worlds of magical sound

within this scared space

love letter

your lips hold back the secrets

that your heart still cannot share

the weight of stories long ago

the shame that you still bear

the silence holds a deadly roar

that strains upon your soul

i see you trapped behind the wall

the darkness swallowed whole

you look at me with agony

you're ready for the light

a shattering of fragile breath

your sense's second sight

i stand beside you reaching out

with tenderness anew

arise my sweet and come to me

your being will renew

the roar is speeding through your body

clawing its way out

it tears through all your suffering

a hoarsely potent shout

it shakes you to your very core

racked with crushing pain

you burst out through your loneliness

your tears a healing rain

you take my hands with fragile calm

we stand in silence shared

you let my heart flow into yours

your anguish fully bared

i hold your soft and battered heart

nestled within my own

a cradle strong and infinite

a love you've always known

rest my love, my own sweet child

a new day will break through

the moon will come with starry skies

and you will live anew

the blessing

when your soul cries out in anguish

and your heart is rife with torment

know that i am always near

with grace and divine intent

call for me in your agony

i am here to hold you close

drawing from angelic energies

pulling you from misery's throes

the light surrounds you always

you shall never walk alone

through troubles and your suffering

dharma carries you home

may the sun draw radiance into your life

the shadows bring depth to your ways

may the abundance of life bring joyful wisdom

may love fill all of your days

thank you

Thank you for reading this little book and I hope you enjoyed it or related to it.

I am so grateful for all the angels in my life and those I meet with each day.
A very special thanks to my mother Nina Khajuria,
who inspired me to write and share this poetry.

May you shine your light bright and strong, beautiful soul!

With love,

PK Davies

about the author

P.K. Davies creates manifesting and mindfulness content at Joyful Life Mastery. Joyful Life Mastery's award-winning tools combine metaphysical magic with down-to-earth goal achievement and a saucy passion for creative growth.

To learn more or sign up for her newsletter, visit JoyfulLifeMastery.com.

She is also the author of the mystery novel *Bollywood P.I. California Dreaming*.

Also by PK Davies:

BOOKS

THE COSMIC PLAYBOOK: 30 Vital Mini Meditations for Love, Hope and Courage

THE COSMIC PLAYBOOK FOR WRITERS: Daily Affirmations and Mindfulness for Writers and Authors

THE LAW OF ATTRACTION GAME BOOK: The Feel Great Handbook

BOLLYWOOD P.I. CALIFORNIA DREAMING: As Priya Khajuria Mystery / Action & Adventure / Humour

MANIFESTING FUN

THE PROSPERITY GAME SUPERKIT

VITAL AFFIRMATIONS
THE SECRET FOREST GUIDED MEDITATION
PURE PEACE MERMAID MEDITATION
GOLDEN EARTH DIVINE HEART ACTIVATION

To explore, visit: **www.Joyfullifemastery.com**

Join Me!

Sign up for the author newsletter at:

JoyfulLifeMastery.com

Receive manifesting tips and launch news.

You can find me here on Facebook:

Facebook.com/joyfullifemastery

On Pinterest:

Pinterest.ca/joyfullifemastery

Amazon Author page:

amazon.com/author/pkdavies

Instagram

https://www.instagram.com/soundismusic/

If you enjoyed this book and believe that someone else will enjoy it and find it helpful, please consider sharing a little blurb wherever you bought it.

Or perhaps recommend it to someone you know who would love it.

Thank you, I appreciate it very much!

www.ingramcontent.com/pod-product-compliance
Lightning Source LLC
Chambersburg PA
CBHW072209100526
44589CB00015B/2447